QUEER JOY
PRIDE
ACE
QUEER EVERYWHERE
YAS QUEER
SLAY
THEY THEM
LEGEND-ARY
404 GENDER NOT FOUND
STONEWALL 1969
QUEER & HERE
YAS QUEEN
BORN THIS WAY
DRAG TIME
SLAY
SLAY
QUEER JOY
PROTECT THE DOLLS
AF584216

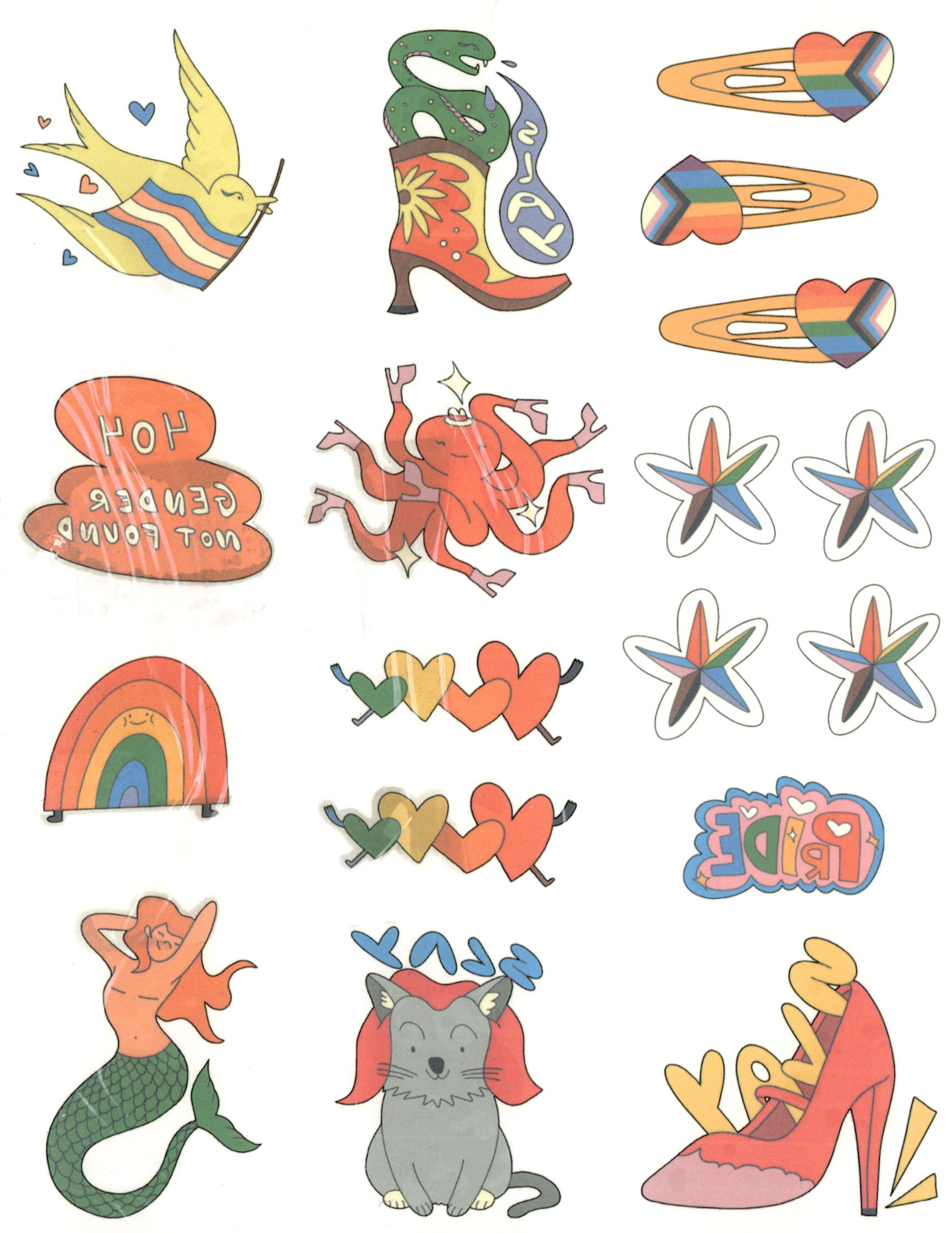
404
GENDER NOT FOUND
PRIDE

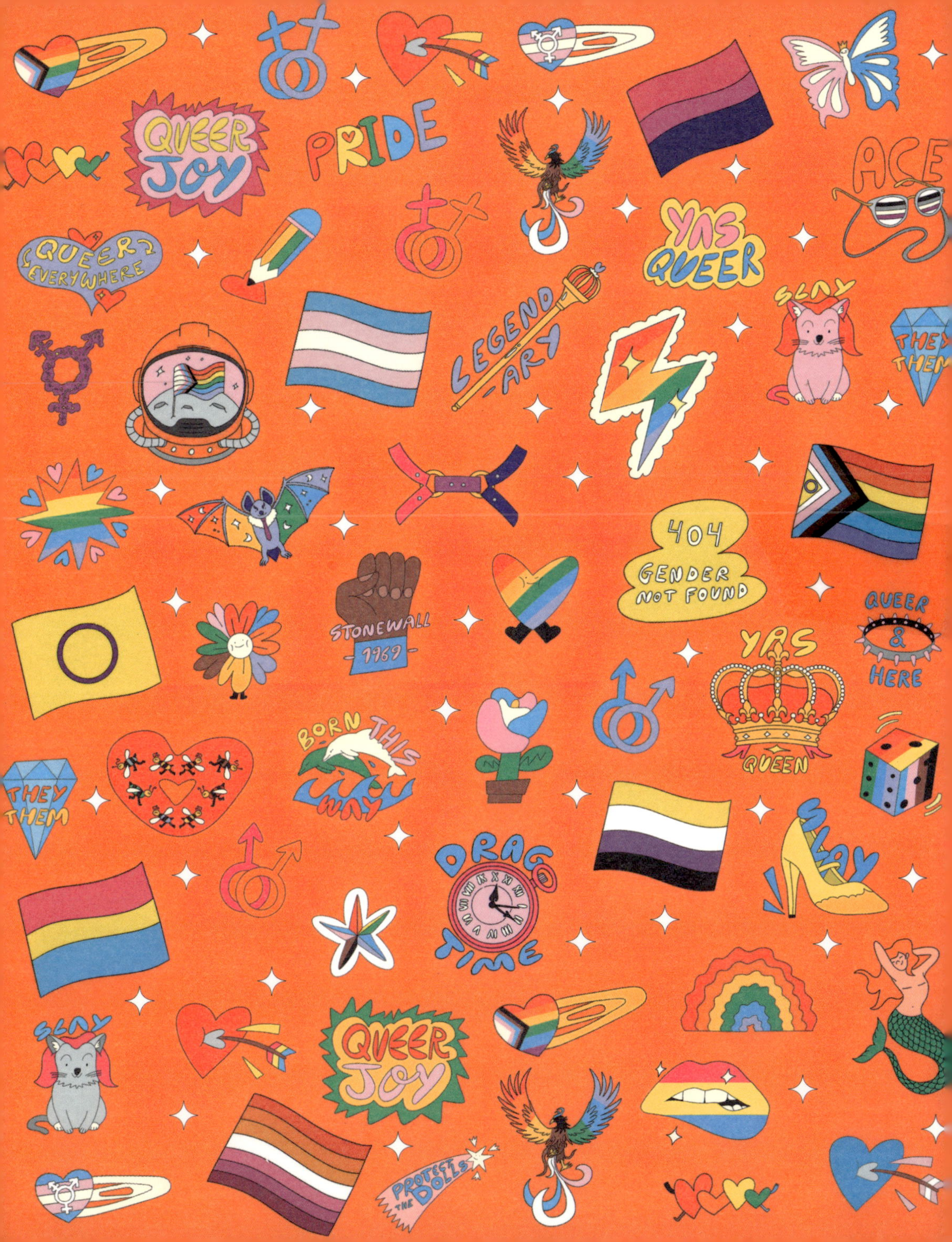

QUEER JOY
PRIDE
ACE
QUEER EVERYWHERE
YAS QUEER
SLAY
LEGENDARY
THEY THEM
404 GENDER NOT FOUND
STONEWALL 1969
QUEER & HERE
YAS QUEEN
BORN THIS WAY
THEY THEM
DRAG TIME
SLAY
SLAY
QUEER JOY
PROTECT THE DOLLS

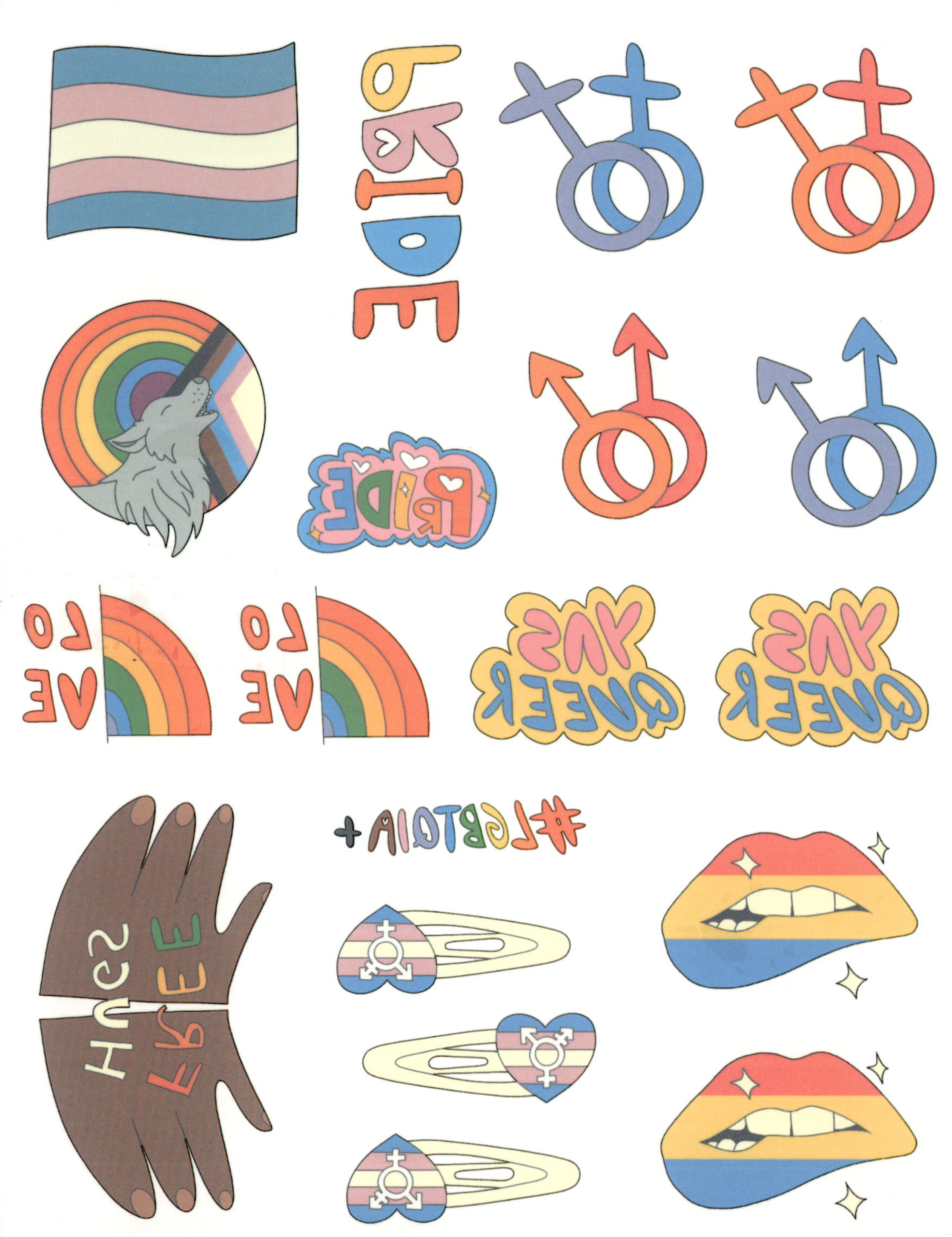
PRIDE
PRIDE
LOVE
LOVE
YAS QUEER
YAS QUEER
#LGBTQIA+
FREE HUGS

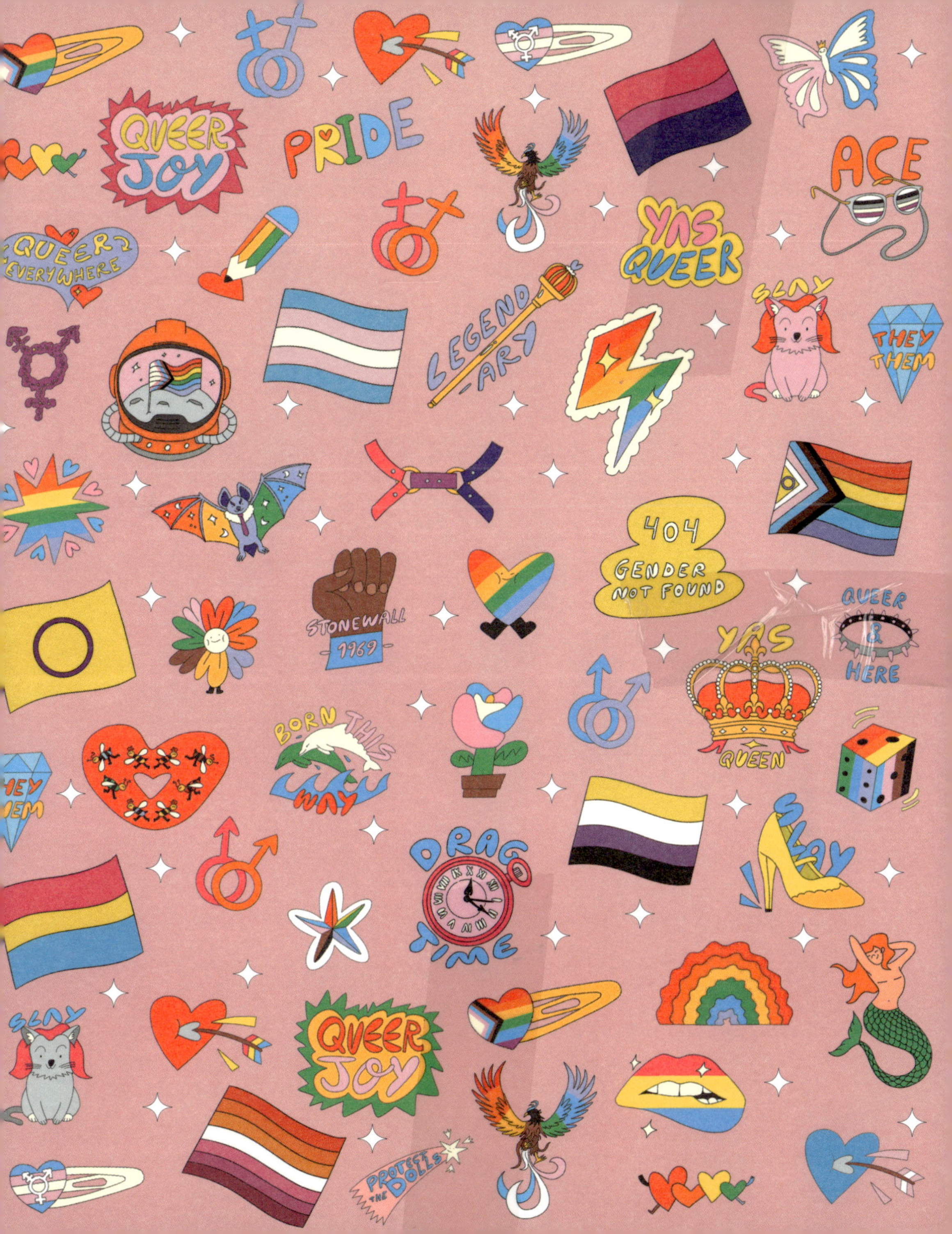
QUEER JOY
PRIDE
ACE
YAS QUEER
QUEER EVERYWHERE
SLAY
THEY THEM
LEGEND-ARY
404 GENDER NOT FOUND
STONEWALL 1969
QUEER & HERE
YAS QUEEN
BORN THIS WAY
DRAG TIME
SLAY
QUEER JOY
SLAY
PROTECT THE DOLLS

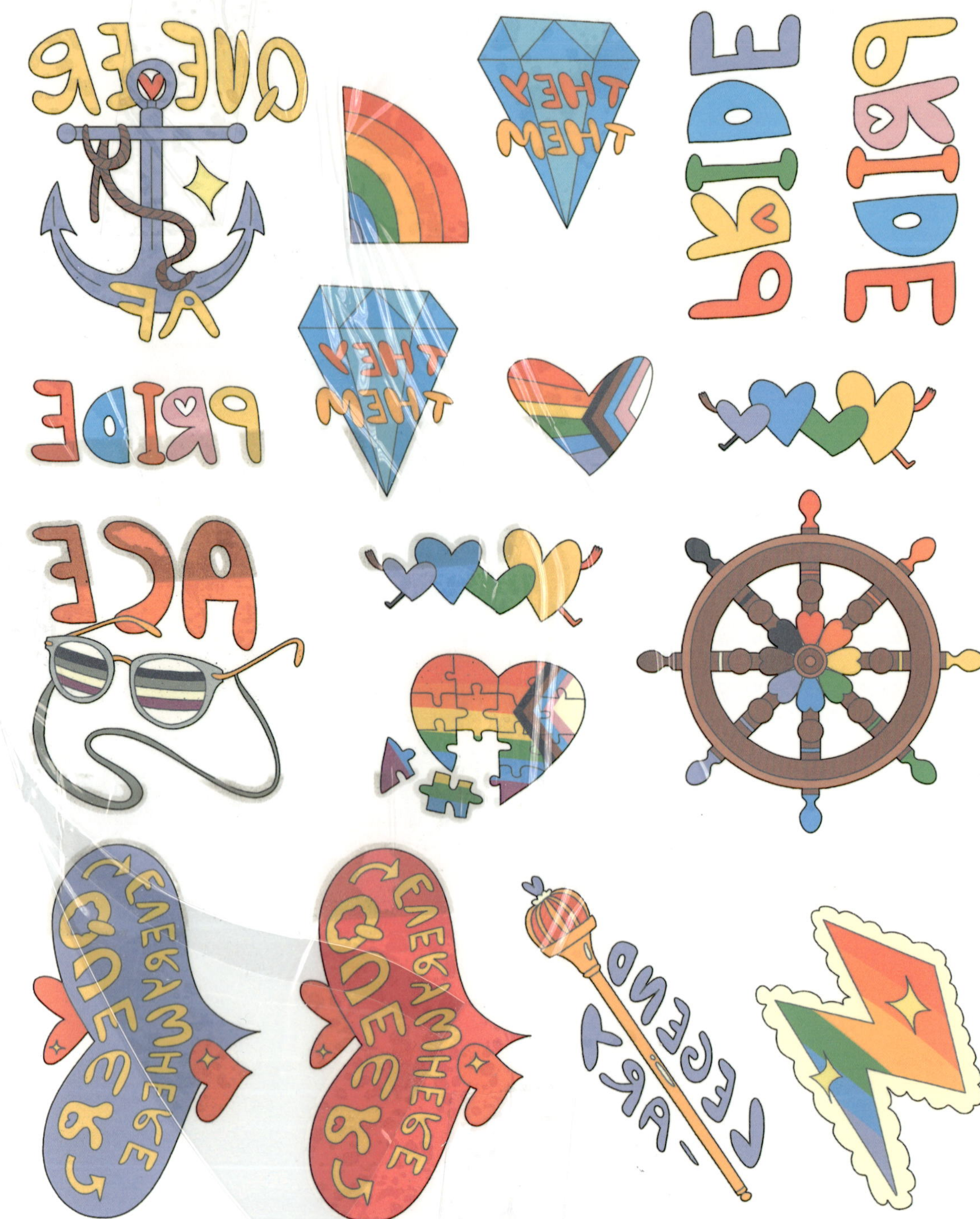

QUEER AF
THEY THEM
PRIDE
ACE
LEGEND-ARY

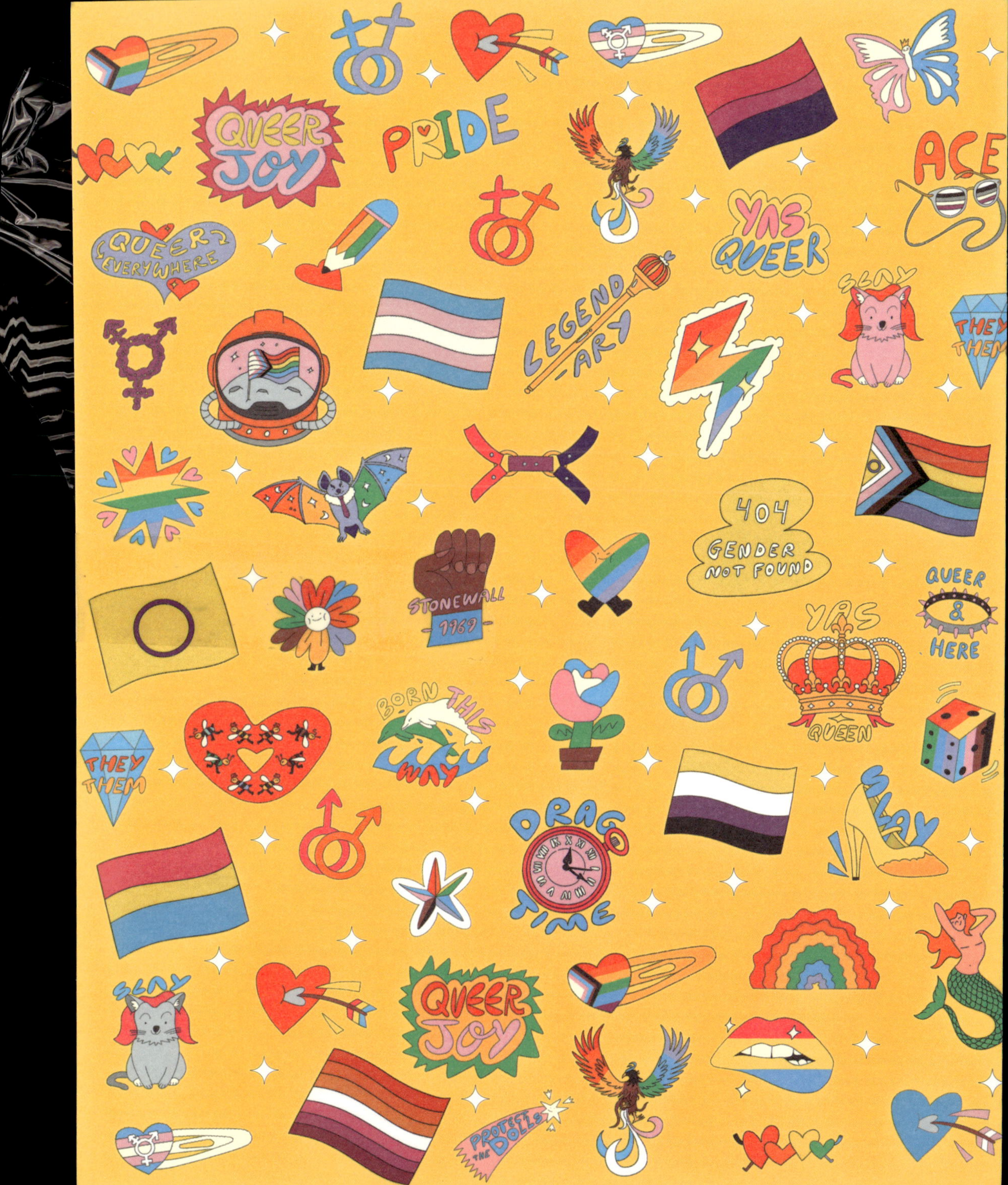
QUEER JOY
PRIDE
ACE
QUEER EVERYWHERE
YAS QUEER
SLAY
LEGEND -ARY
THEY THEM
404 GENDER NOT FOUND
STONEWALL 1969
QUEER & HERE
YAS
QUEEN
BORN THIS WAY
THEY THEM
DRAG TIME
SLAY
SLAY
QUEER JOY
PROTECT THE DOLLS

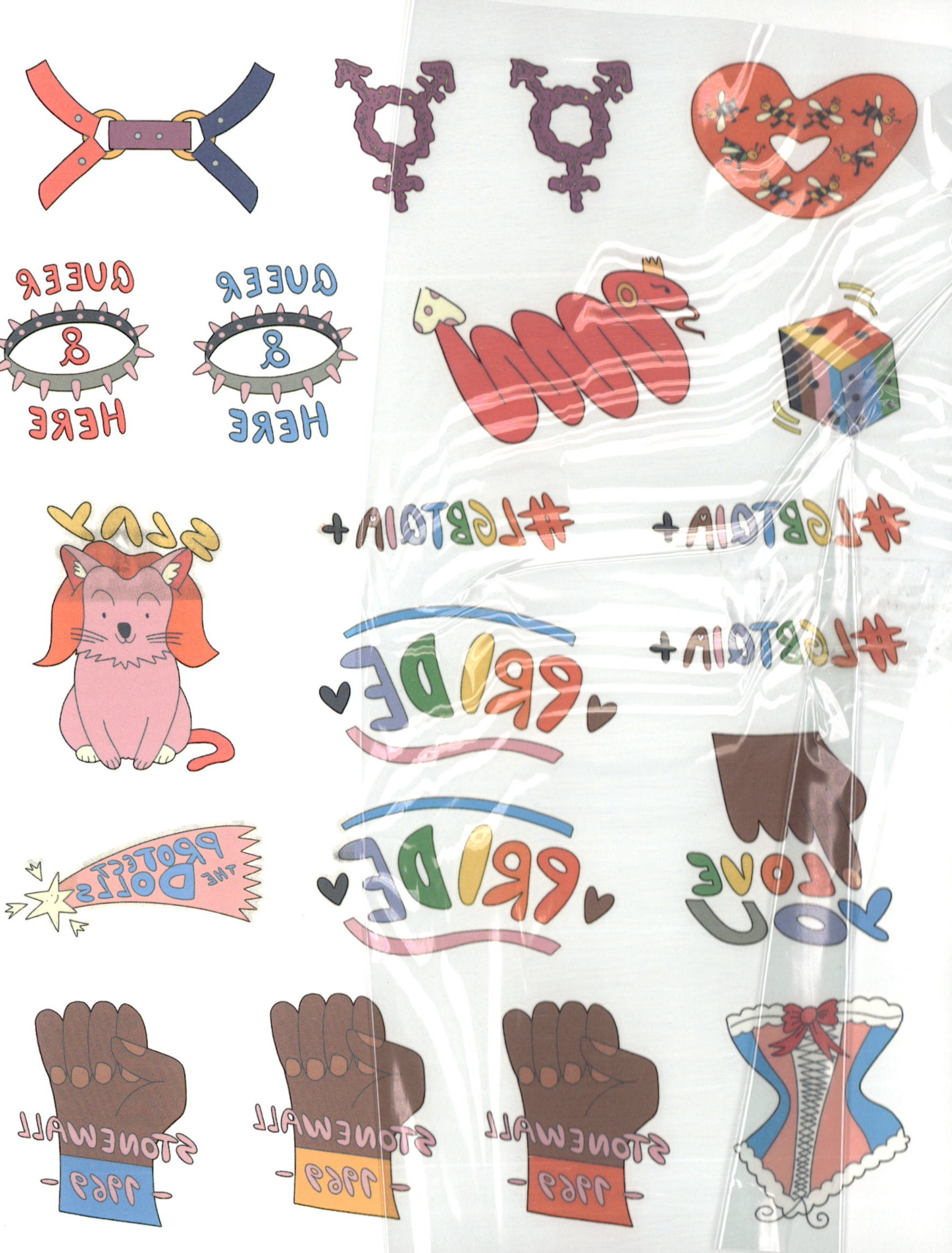
QUEER
&
HERE
QUEER
&
HERE
SLAY
#LGBTQIA+
#LGBTQIA+
#LGBTQIA+
PRIDE
PRIDE
PROTECT THE DOLLS
LOVE YOU
STONEWALL
1969
STONEWALL
1969
STONEWALL
1969

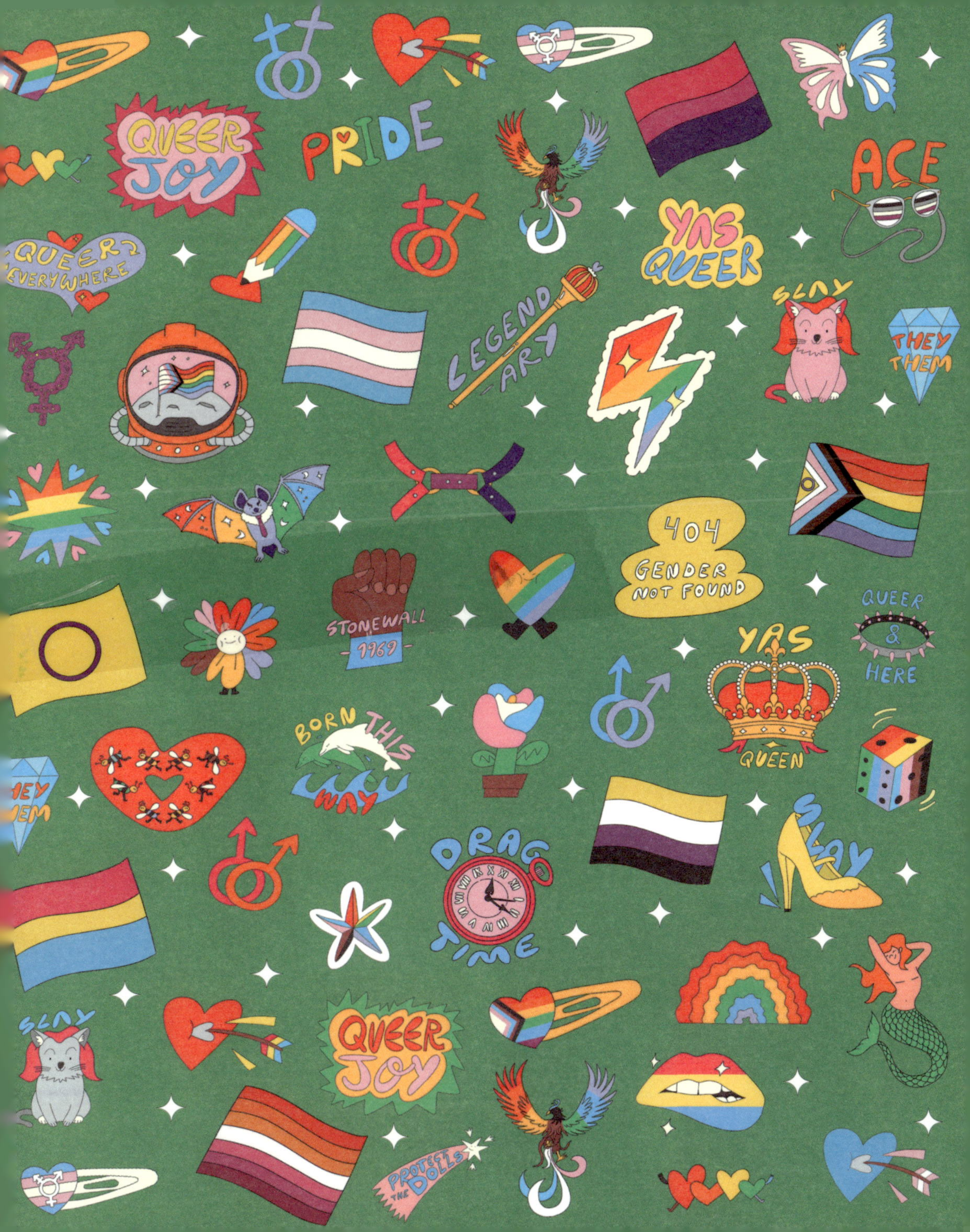

QUEER JOY
PRIDE
QUEERS EVERYWHERE
ACE
YAS QUEER
SLAY
LEGEND-ARY
THEY THEM
404 GENDER NOT FOUND
QUEER & HERE
STONEWALL 1969
YAS QUEEN
BORN THIS WAY
DRAG TIME
SLAY
SLAY
QUEER JOY
PROTECT THE DOLLS

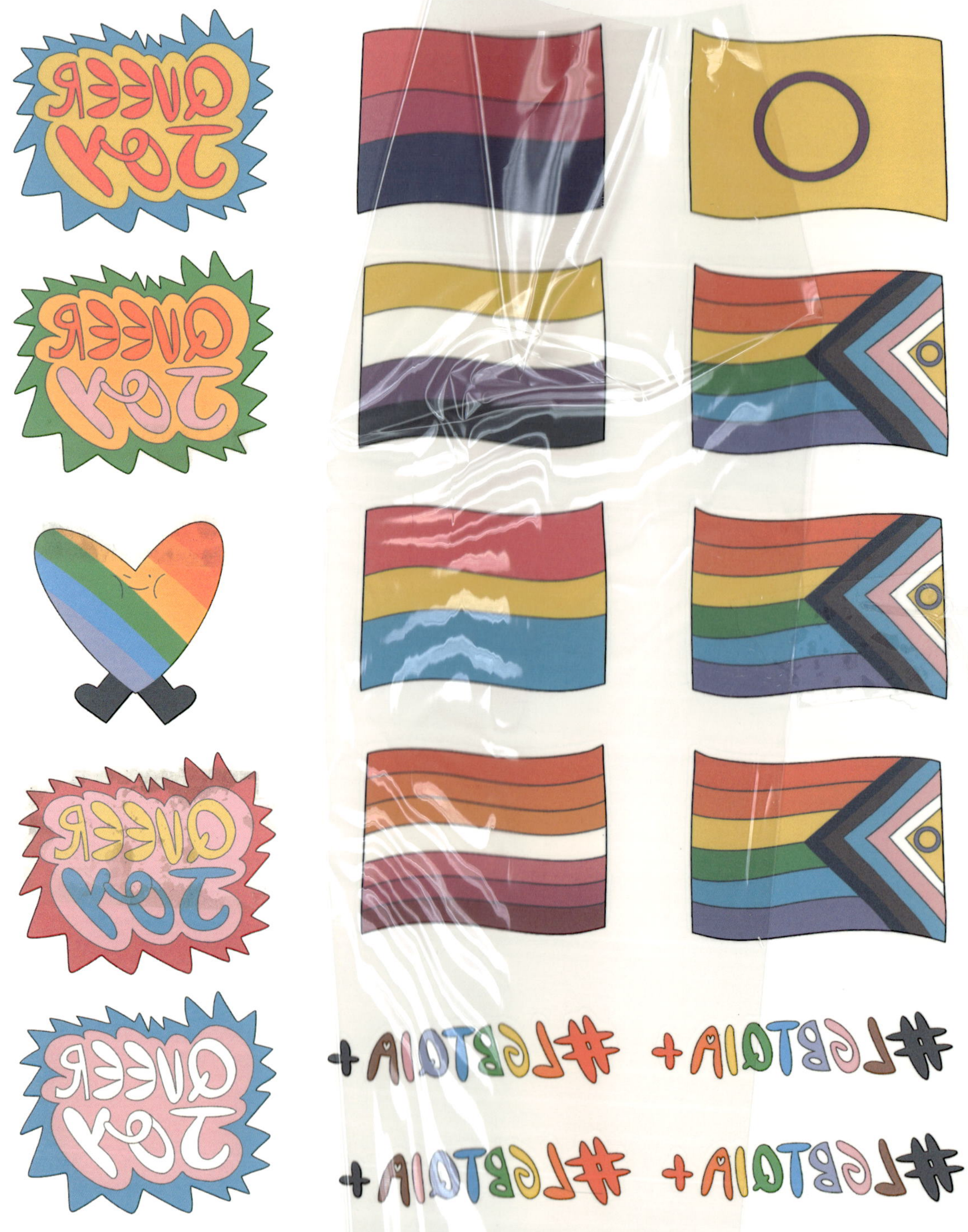
QUEER JOY
QUEER JOY
QUEER JOY
QUEER JOY
#LGBTQIA+
#LGBTQIA+
#LGBTQIA+
#LGBTQIA+

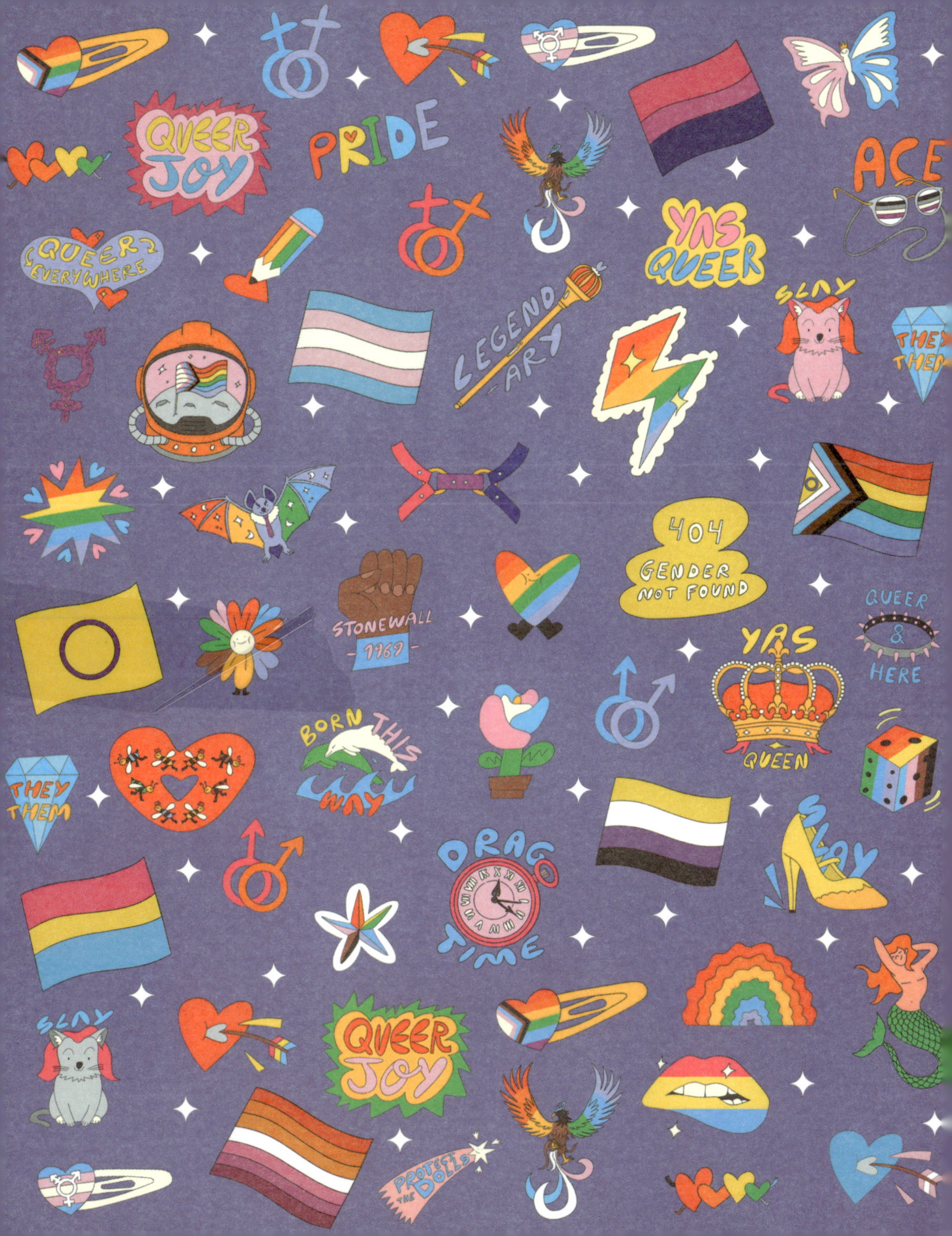
QUEER JOY
PRIDE
ACE
QUEER EVERYWHERE
YAS QUEER
SLAY
LEGEND-ARY
THEY THEM
404 GENDER NOT FOUND
STONEWALL
1969
QUEER & HERE
YAS
QUEEN
BORN THIS WAY
THEY THEM
DRAG TIME
SLAY
SLAY
QUEER JOY
PROTECT THE DOLLS

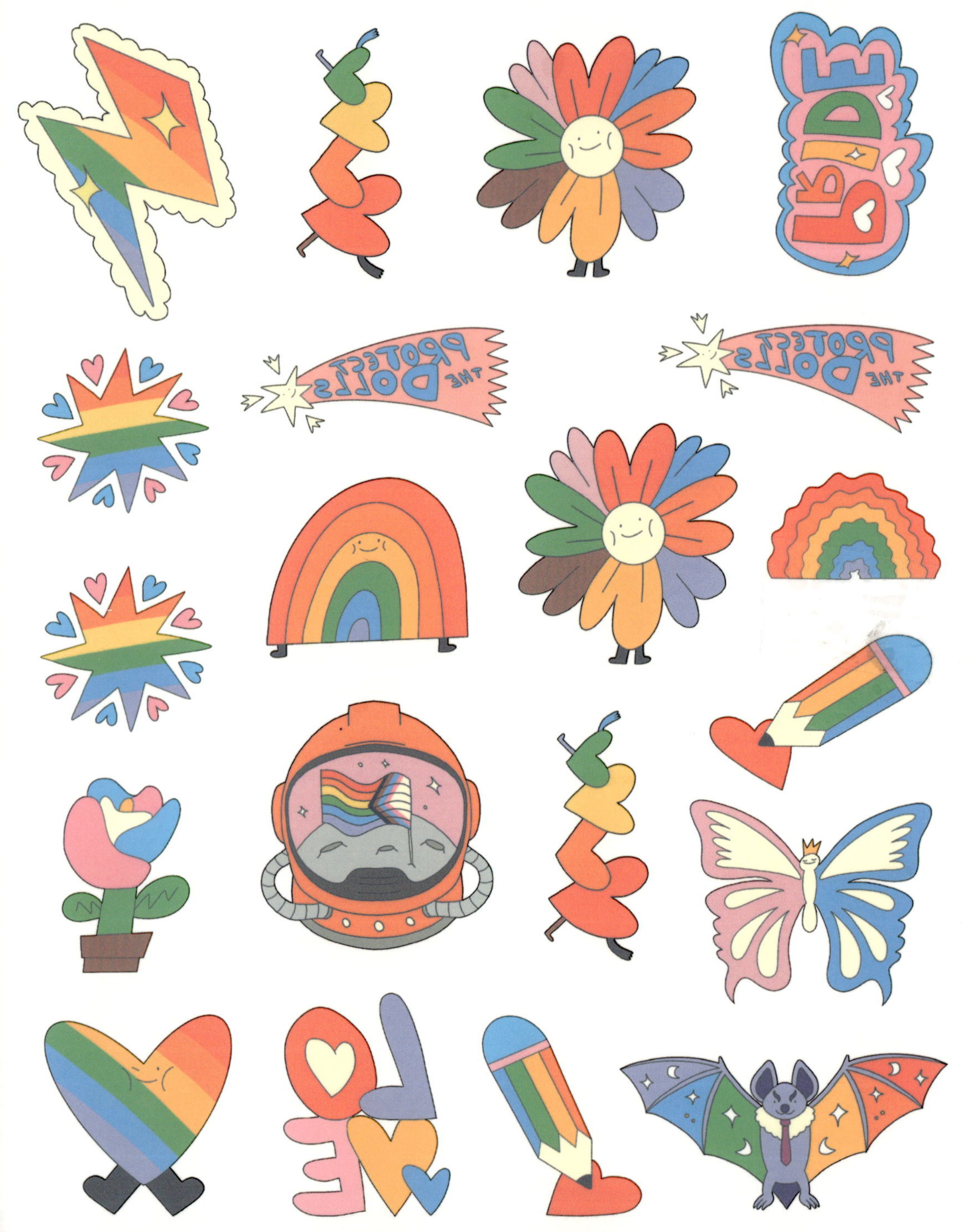
PRIDE
PROTECT THE DOLLS
PROTECT THE DOLLS
LOVE

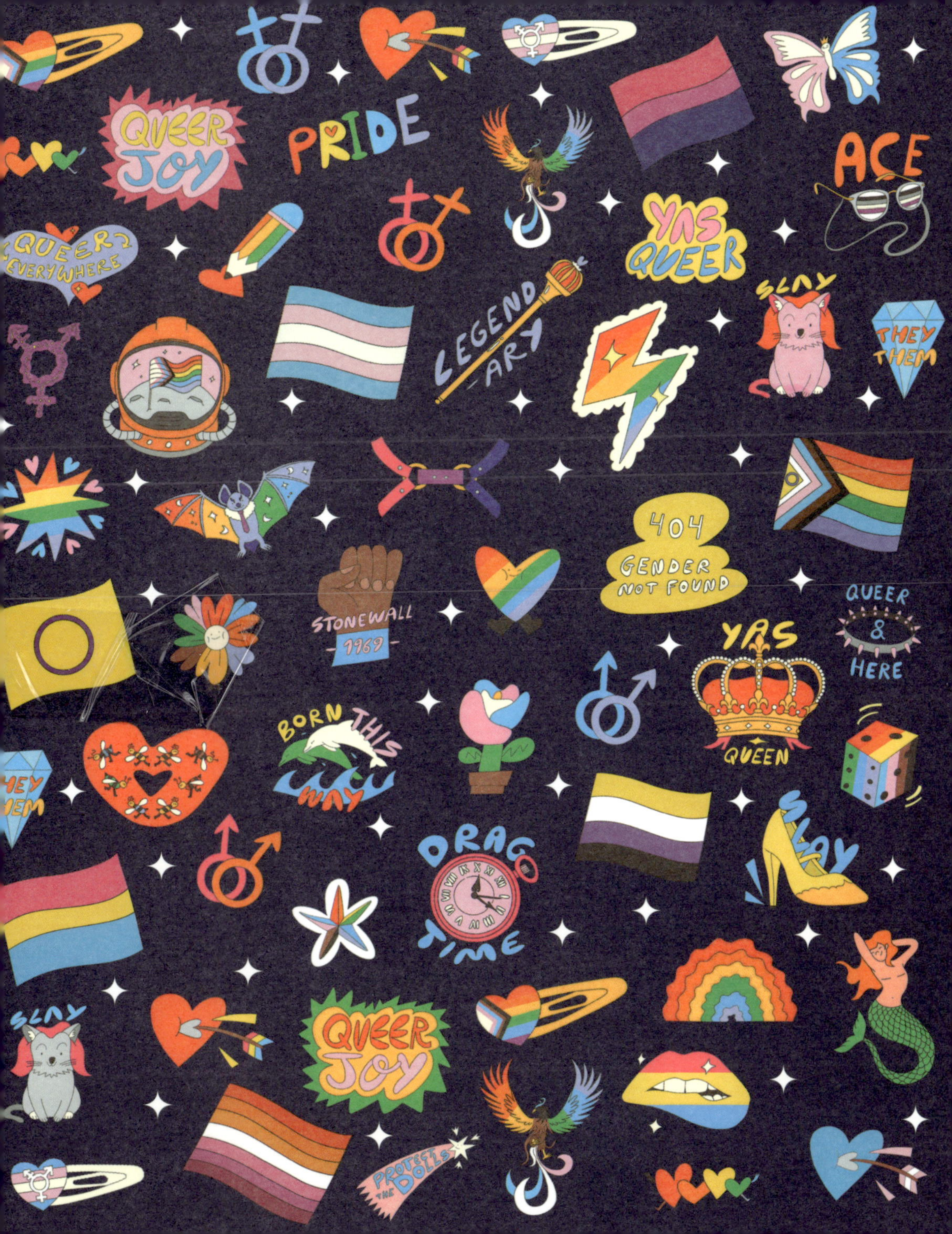
QUEER JOY
PRIDE
ACE
QUEERS EVERYWHERE
YAS QUEER
SLAY
LEGEND -ARY
THEY THEM
404 GENDER NOT FOUND
STONEWALL 1969
QUEER & HERE
YAS QUEEN
BORN THIS WAY
DRAG TIME
SLAY
SLAY
QUEER JOY
PROTECT THE DOLLS

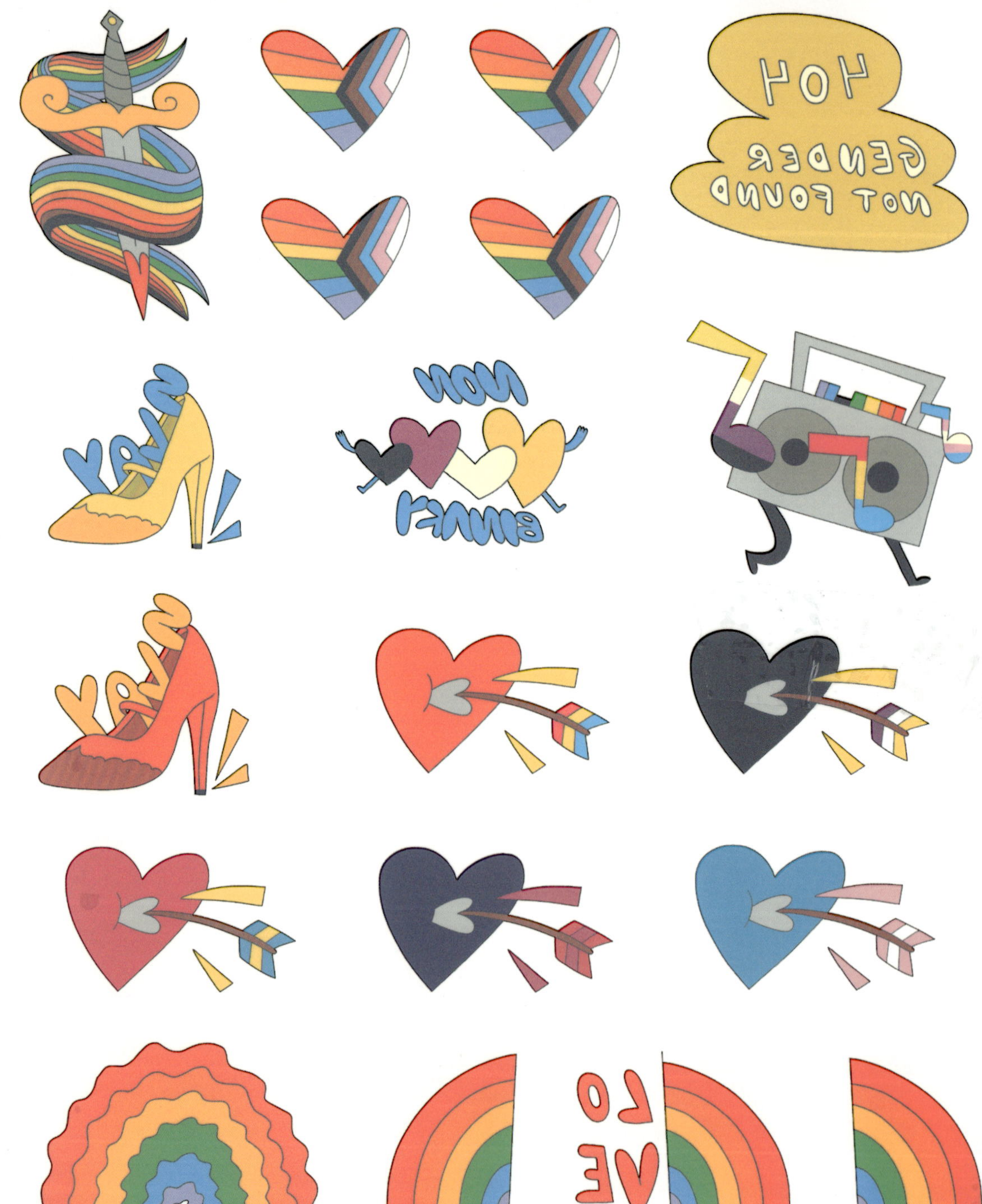
404
GENDER
NOT FOUND
SLAY
NON
BINARY
SLAY
LO
VE

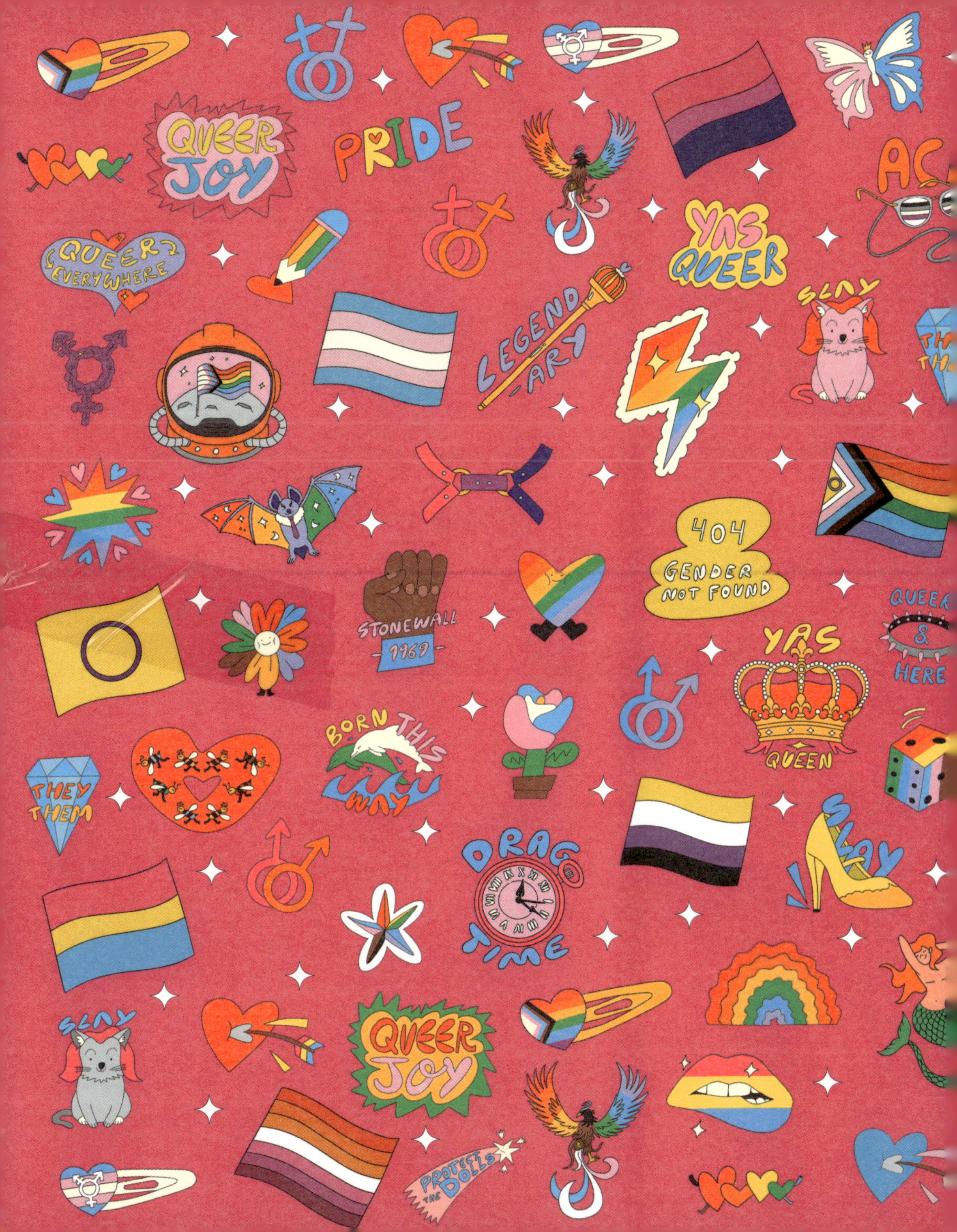

QUEER JOY
PRIDE
QUEER EVERYWHERE
YAS QUEER
LEGENDARY
SLAY
404 GENDER NOT FOUND
STONEWALL 1969
QUEER & HERE
YAS QUEEN
BORN THIS WAY
THEY THEM
DRAG TIME
SLAY
SLAY
QUEER JOY
PROTECT THE DOLLS

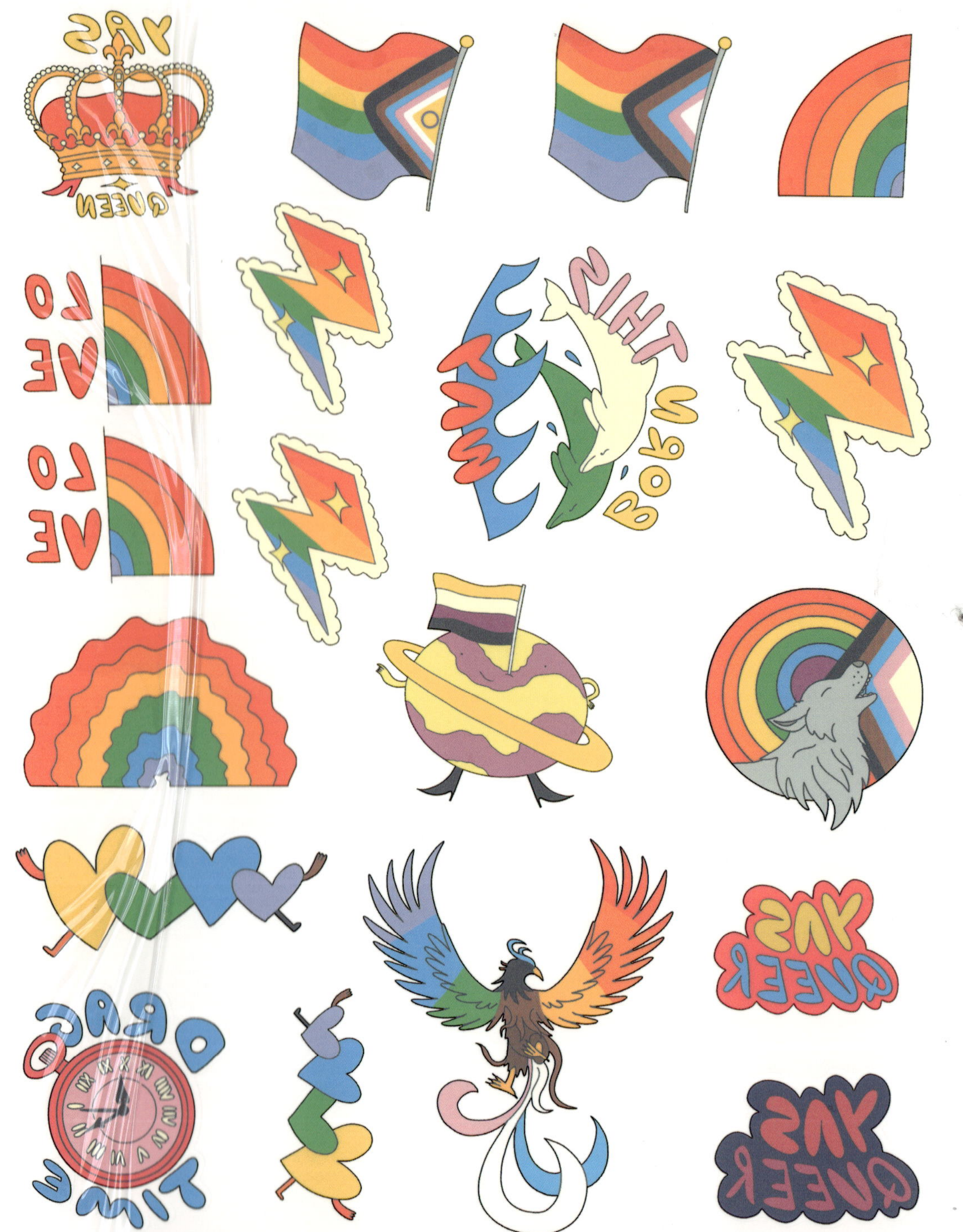
YAS QUEEN
LO VE
LO VE
BORN THIS WAY
YAS QUEER
DRAG TIME
YAS QUEER